FREE HEARTS

Understanding Your Deepest Motivations

FREE HEARTS

Understanding Your Deepest Motivations

Alexandre Havard

Author of Virtuous Leadership, Created for Greatness, *and* From Temperament to Character

Copyright © 2020 by Alexandre Havard. Translated from French by Anthony Salvia

Alexandre Havard is the author of three previous books: *Virtuous Leadership: An Agenda for Personal Excellence* (2007), *Created for Greatness: The Power of Magnanimity* (2014), and *From Temperament to Character: On Becoming a Virtuous Leader* (2018), all published in English by Scepter Publishers.

Scripture texts from the New and Old Testaments are taken from The Holy Bible Revised Standard Catholic Edition © 1965 and 1966 by the Division of Christian Education of the National Council of the Churches of Christ in the United States. All rights reserved. All copyrighted material is used by permission of the copyright owner. No part of it may be reproduced without permission in writing from the copyright owner.

This edition of *FREE HEARTS* is © 2020 by Scepter Publishers, Inc.
info@scepterpublishers.org
www.scepterpublishers.org
800 322 8773
New York

All rights reserved. The total or partial reproduction of this book is not permitted, nor its informatic treatment, or the transmission of any form or by any means, either electronic, mechanic, photocopy, or other methods without written permission of the copyright owner.

Cover image: *Sunrise over the Eastern Sea* by Fujishima Takeji. Alamy.com.
Interior images: Alamy.com

Cover, text design, and pagination by Carol Sawyer, Rose Design

Book ISBN: 978-1-59417-395-0
eBook ISBN: 978-1-59417-396-7

Library of Congress number: 2020941400

Printed in the United States of America

Contents

Preface.. vii
From the Author... xi

1 The Heart: Source and Center........................... 1
2 The Spirituality of the Heart............................. 7
3 The Rationalist... 15
4 The Religious Voluntarist................................. 23
5 The Macho Voluntarist.................................... 27
6 The Ideological Voluntarist............................... 31
7 The Conventional Voluntarist............................ 35
8 The Voluptuous Sentimentalist.......................... 39
9 The Insane Sentimentalist................................ 43
10 The Cowardly Sentimentalist............................ 47
11 Desiccated Hearts... 51

12 Wounded Hearts 57
13 Beauty 61
14 Greatness 71
15 Love 77
16 Freedom 81
17 Mercy 87
18 Suffering 93

Conclusion 97

Preface

July 2013, Mombasa, Kenya.

Seven years ago, the president of Kenya's Commission for the Implementation of the Constitution invited me to present my virtuous leadership system to some fifty deputies, senators, and governors and to take questions.

It was the first time I had ever addressed an audience of politicians. Gerald Otieno Kajwang rose to his feet.

A famous senator, Kajwang was a huge, strapping man who engaged more than once in physical brawls with other politicians. He was known for his sense of humor.

He grabbed the microphone: "Alexandre, you are preaching to the wrong public. We are politicians precisely because we are not virtuous people. All of us here are bandits, and perhaps even criminals. That is our job."

I was taken aback by his sincerity, but managed to retort: "Sir, the fact that you are a bandit and a criminal is not the problem."

Stupefied, Kajwang fell back into his chair.

"No, the problem is not that you are bad. The problem is that you are small. The problem of evil is not the evil itself. It is the diminution of the person, the shrinking of the heart, the stunting of the spirit it entails, and the damage this provokes. Your problem is the diminution of your being; I am here to help you fix this problem because a small person is an ugly person."

Kajwang kept a humble silence. A year later, at 55, he died of cardiac arrest.

I learned in a roundabout way that he had changed profoundly after our meeting. He had grasped the meaning of the basic principles of morality not through a class on the Ten Commandments but through aesthetics and a true vision of the human heart.

Kajwang had converted his heart.

A good friend of mine—the dean of Kenya's Strathmore Law School—invited Kajwang to speak to his students a few weeks prior to his death. My friend knew him well. He told me Kajwang had undergone a powerful transformation. He had become humble and reflective. He was rethinking his whole life. This reflective period had utterly changed him.

Many are prepared to reconcile themselves to the thought that they are personally bad and ill-intentioned. They can live with that. But few are content to be thought of as ugly and to live in the knowledge that their hearts are shriveled.

The education of the heart is what we need if we want to soar like eagles rather than flap about like barnyard fowl.

From the Author

I have written several books aimed at promoting virtue in leadership in which the heart is prominently featured. And yet I felt the need to author a new book that focuses exclusively on the heart's role in leadership, because the subject is that important. Why?

Because, as I observed in my first book,[1] leadership is virtue in action and virtue is a habit of the heart as much as it is of the intellect and the will. In fact, before the will and the intellect even begin to practice virtue, the heart needs to *desire* virtue. The heart must come to contemplate and prize virtue if it is to become a stable orientation toward action. And it must be a *value* in the hearts of leaders if they are to embrace virtue as a dynamic force

---

1. Alexandre Havard, *Virtuous Leadership: An Agenda for Personal Excellence* (New York: Scepter, 2008).

in their professional and personal lives. Thus, the heart is nothing less than the foundation of virtue.

Magnanimity and humility, which are virtues of the heart *par excellence*, are the essence of leadership. Whereas prudence, courage, self-mastery, and justice—all virtues of the intellect and the will—are its foundation. A deeper knowledge of the heart will help us to practice magnanimity and humility more consequentially, thereby becoming better leaders, and, in fact, true leaders.

A second question may arise: With so much in contemporary social and political life being determined and steered by feelings and passions, often to the detriment of rational discussion, why write a book about the heart now, amidst the aggressive sentimentalism in which we are living? Why speak in defense of the heart, when the heart invariably trumps the intellect and the will? The heart has become so omnipotent that it would hardly seem to need an advocate.

I would say that *in the name of the Heart* we eliminated the heart, in the same way French Jacobins, Bolsheviks, and abortionists eliminated millions of human beings in the name of Man. Why? Because our vision of man and our vision of the heart are perverted. We do not understand the real workings of a human being.

It is more necessary than ever to speak about the heart and to tell the truth about it. An exalted and exalting truth. The heart refers not just to feelings produced by the (often selfish) demands of the flesh but also to sentiments produced by God in the depths of our being. In this sense, the heart cannot be isolated from the intellect and the will: man's spiritual self is a unified reality.

In a world infested by feel-good quackery, I felt the need to tell the whole truth about the heart.

But why then "free hearts"? Why do I need to develop not merely a good heart or a great heart, but a *free* heart?

A good heart is full of good intentions. A great heart is full of good intentions *and* does good deeds. A free heart is something different. It is a heart endowed with an extraordinary power: the power to consistently perceive the highest realities of life, even if invisible (sensibility), and respond straight away to those realities (responsiveness).

Let me explain.

When we speak of freedom, we usually have in mind the freedom of the will. By freedom we mean that, unlike an animal whose will is determined by instinct, we can make choices.

Beyond this *basic liberty*—this free will—however, there exists a superior liberty—a liberty of the heart. A free heart is a heart accustomed to saying "yes" to transcendent values, to the impulses and divine inspirations that manifest themselves in the depths of our being. Our degree of freedom depends on the frequency and intensity with which we say "yes."

Freedom of the heart is more difficult to achieve than freedom of the will. We need to work intensely on our interior selves. It is about much more than just *doing something*; it is all about *letting go*. It is about letting ourselves be touched, thrilled, embraced by that which is greater than us. In short, it is about letting ourselves be loved by God. Letting ourselves be loved should be the main task of our life.

Free Hearts will help us:

- Achieve the optimal balance between the heart, the mind, and the will
- Heal our heart when it is troubled and has been wounded, and
- Enable our most noble sentiments and aspirations to attain new strength and maturity.

January 29, 2020

CHAPTER 1

The Heart: Source and Center

The human being possesses three **centers** of freedom and responsibility: reason, the will and the heart. Reason and the will are exclusively spiritual faculties. The heart is spiritual and physical at the same time.

These centers are not independent. They can only be developed together. If one of the three elements is isolated from the others, it corrupts itself and the totality of the human organism. Rationalism (the exclusive emphasis on reason), voluntarism (the exclusive emphasis on the will) and sentimentalism (the exclusive emphasis on the heart) paralyze man and make him unhappy.

The heart, because it is a power at once spiritual and physical, is the most complex but also the richest part of the human personality. Man is worth what his heart is worth. His heart is his most intimate "I." It is his heart which experiences happiness, not his intellect or his will.

The heart is the source of physical and psychic life. It is also the source of spiritual life: the heart is, as Blaise Pascal said, the foundation of reason and the will.

The heart is the foundation of reason: it immediately and intuitively captures the *existence* of things which cannot logically be proved.[1] The heart establishes therefore the point of departure for reasoning and knowledge.

The heart is also the foundation of the will: it presents immediately and intuitively *the aims* of our existence which give direction to the will (the fundamental choice we make, often unconsciously, between the Creator and creatures, between God and "me"). A person without a heart does not exist, nor one whose heart is empty, because it cannot be empty. It is always full. It holds the good (vision, drive) and the evil (blindness, impotence), and if the good decreases, the bad increases.

---

[1]. The heart sometimes grasps the *essence* of things (what is this thing?), but never fails to grasp the *existence* of things (does this thing exist in reality?).

The heart is not only the personality's source but its center, and the center of affections. "For where your treasure is, there will your heart be also."[2]

The heart is also the center of our relationship with God: it is mainly in a person's heart that God acts, even if he also acts—secondarily—in the mind and the will. The heart is the organ of communion between man and God. "God is closer to us than we are to ourselves," affirms St. Augustine, because God alone knows what is happening in the depths of our heart and the sincerity with which we are responding to his inspirations.

The heart occupies a privileged place in poetry, literature, and religion (in particular, the Bible), as well as certain traditions, like the Russian one. Pyotr Chaadaev, Vladimir Soloviev, Pavel Florensky: These philosophers witnessed (by their lives no less than through their writings) the importance of the heart. By contrast, in classical Greek and Western philosophy (with exceptions like St. Augustine, Blaise Pascal, and Dietrich von Hildebrand), the heart is poorly valued. The place it occupies, if it occupies one at all, beside the mind and the will, is almost irrelevant.

Although he wrote some very beautiful things about love, Plato, in his philosophical system, accords the mind a unique and exorbitant place. Aristotle, although he

---

2. Mt 6:21.

affirms that the truly virtuous man feels joy when he practices virtue, puts the accent only on the intellect and the will. The heart, for him, is not a spiritual faculty. It is limited to the physiological and psychical spheres, to the irrational world which man shares with animals.

The philosophy of the ancient Greeks transfers the spiritual attributes of the heart to the intelligence and the will.

Before the West discovered Aristotle, it was St. Augustine—author of the *Confessions*—who provided intellectual guidance. For him, the heart is a faculty both physical and spiritual, even if he refuses to grant it a value on par with reason and the will. Aristotle and his minimalist vision of the heart set the tone in Europe from the twelfth century on. Only with Pascal in the seventeenth century does "the question of the heart" come to the fore. Unfortunately, it was not Pascal, but René Descartes, his contemporary, who made the West what it has become. Descartes has no interest in the heart because it cannot demonstrate *mathematically* the truth of its certainties. Only reason counts—more precisely, *mathematical* reason. Here, we fall into rationalist fanaticism. If Plato and Aristotle failed to "discover" the heart, Descartes takes note of it only to obliterate it by ignoring it straight away.

Be that as it may, the West has emphasized the mind and the will in the life of man, whereas the East has paid greater attention to the heart. The West often accuses the East of sentimentalism, and the East often reproaches the West for its rationalism and voluntarism. Both approaches are false if they do not take into account this elementary fact: the heart, the mind, and the will can only function together. One can only practice the good with a pure heart, an enlightened intelligence, and a strong will.

CHAPTER 2

The Spirituality of the Heart

Human affectivity in its physiological and psychic dimensions resembles animal affectivity. Men, like animals, experience such positive feelings as love, desire, pleasure, hope, and audacity, and such negative ones as hatred, aversion, sorrow, despair, fear, and anger.[1]

The affectivity experienced by animals has no moral ramifications. This is not true of human beings. Human

---

1. In Western cultures, these feelings are often called "passions," whereas in the East "passions" refer exclusively to the perverse inclinations of human nature. To avoid confusion, I will not use the word "passion."

feelings and emotions are morally qualified (they can be called "good" or "bad") as soon as they engage reason and the will. The anger I feel when someone runs off with my wife is good and justified, but when someone thwarts my plan to run off with *his* wife, my anger is bad.

Our virtues ennoble our emotions, our vices corrupt them.

Men, like animals, inevitably experience feelings of a psychic kind. But in contrast to animals, they can also experience superior kinds of feelings: a holy enthusiasm, disinterested love, deep gratitude, profound contrition, sincere pardon, active compassion, a just wrath at the injustice being inflicted on another.

One easily perceives the difference between feelings of a psychical kind, common to human beings and animals, and superior feelings of a spiritual kind, appropriate only to humans. We may call these feelings "sentiments."

A sentiment of the spiritual order is the fruit of a response of the heart to certain *values* which touch us in the depth of our being. The emotion provoked in us by extraordinary virtue or beauty perceived in nature or in art is an emotion which engages our freedom. The emotion produced is a consequence of the "yes" that the heart pronounces, of the often-unconscious acquiescence we make to the good when it seizes us. Such a response transforms us interiorly and exalts us. It lays the foundation of virtue because, before being a dynamic force, virtue should be for us a *value*. Before being a habit that we practice, a noble capacity and stable orientation toward action, virtue should be *contemplated and prized*. Before being practiced, it should be *desired*.

As Dietrich von Hildebrand wrote: "A person can develop all the spiritual richness to which he is called only if he is penetrated, imbibed by the values which he perceives and only if his heart is stirred and inflamed by these values and responds to them with the fire of joy, enthusiasm and love."[2]

A humble person lets himself be easily moved and is not ashamed of his emotions.

Spiritual affectivity is *transcendent* because it puts us in contact with realities greater than ourselves. It is not a question of spiritualizing emotions of the physiological or psychical type: it is a question of experiencing spiritual or transcendent emotions which transform, purify, and inflame us.

---

2. Dietrich von Hildebrand, *The Heart* (Chicago: Franciscan Herald Press, 1977), p. 97.

Freedom is the quality of a heart accustomed to saying "yes" to transcendent values. The "yes" demands the humility which predisposes us to be attentive to the calls of beauty, truth, and the good. The proud person resists being moved by transcendent values because nothing in this world exceeds himself. He thinks he should do the moving. Pride is the greatest obstacle to the education of the heart.

The more reason and will engage in the heart's response to transcendent values, the more this response will be spiritual. But it is the heart that has initial, privileged access to values. One need only observe the behavior of infants: they perceive many things, but only with the heart. Its education begins in the mother's womb, well before the education of their intelligence and the will. And the traces left by the education of the heart on our personality are much deeper than those left by the education of the will and the mind.

Man is greater than the sum of his knowledge or the things he can control by his will. His being enters mysterious depths that go far beyond what he can know and what he can do. God produces sacred things—great intuitions, exalted feelings, holy emotions—in the heart of the humble person. These sacred things are a gratuitous gift of the Creator.

The depths of the heart are not the depths of the subconscious. The depths of the heart are mystical: the communion between the Creator, his creatures, and the created world. The subconscious depths are psychological and incommunicable.

For one reason or another, it can happen that for more or less long periods of our life our affectivity, or perception, becomes "anesthetized." The heart seems dead: it is cold and dry. The sixteenth-century Spanish mystic, Saint John of the Cross, called this phenomenon "The dark night of the soul."[3]

It is undeniably an existential experience which purifies us radically of all sentimentality: we no longer enjoy our emotions because we no longer have emotions. But to desire entering the night of the soul is madness! God did not create us in order to amputate us. The normal path to perfection is that of King David: "My heart and flesh sing for joy to the living God."[4]

Our capacity to be moved by goodness and beauty is a strength and not a weakness on our path to perfection.

---

3. Saint John of the Cross, *Ascent of Mount Carmel* (New York: Cosimo, 2007), p. 9.
4. Ps 84:2.

St. Pope John Paul II, the first Slav pope, possessed an extraordinary potential for affectivity—to such a degree that a professor friend called him the most erotic pope in history. He was referring to platonic eroticism, the sublime emotion which arises through contact with tangible beauty and elevates the soul so that it attains the enjoyment of celestial grace.

John Paul II was not afraid of his affective capital because he had learned to love people in the heart of Christ. In the beauty of people he discovered the beauty of God.

We should not fear our capacity for affectivity. We should fear loving people or things with a love other than that of Jesus Christ. Only the heart of Christ can protect us from the affective deviations brought about by original sin, in particular concupiscence. "Love and do what you want," said Saint Augustine.[5] Before doing what we want to do, it is important to be sure that we love as Christ loves: that we love in the heart of Christ. For that, we must practice the virtue of sincerity—with God, with ourselves, and with others.

---

5. Saint Augustine, *Ten Homilies on the Epistle of John to the Parthians*, Treatise VII, 8 (*https://www.sermonindex.net/modules/bible_books/?view=book_chapter&chapter=31529*).

"Create in me a clean heart, O God."[6] The purification of the heart is a life-long process that does not end, just as the effort to submit our intelligence and will to the divine intelligence and will must never cease.

In any case, it is often harder to accept the injunction of the Heart of Jesus than the commandments of his law. When Christ condemned divorce, no one abandoned him, even if many felt his teaching on this point was too much to bear. But when he affirmed that his Body and Blood were indispensable food for the soul, the crowds revolted and left him for good. Their hearts were sick—sicker than their minds. The rich young man who obeyed the commandments from his earliest days did not understand this *radicalism of the heart*: When Jesus invited him to follow him exclusively at the price of abandoning his riches, he fled. His heart failed him more than his will.

Christ makes more demands on our heart than he does on our mind or our will. God wants us to give him our heart. We should *submit* our mind and our will to his, but we must *give* him our heart, which is our true self.

---

6. Ps 51:10.

Suffering leaves the rationalist cold. *The Last Supper* (detail), *Giotto, the Scrovegni Chapel, Padua.*

CHAPTER 3

The Rationalist

A heart smothered by reason: this is rationalism. A heart smothered by the will: this is voluntarism. The heart which smothers both the intellect and the will: this is sentimentalism.

Smothered or smothering hearts are unbalanced. Their poor functioning proceeds from the absence of harmonious communion with the intellect and the will.

Sometimes the heart is smothered by the intellect. This is the case for people for whom life situations are nothing but occasions for broadening their knowledge. Nothing touches them, nothing affects them. They are eternal spectators, like tourists stimulated by curiosity. Only with difficulty do they respond to life circumstances with joy, sadness, compassion, or love. What interests them is intellectual analysis. In reality, the distance they keep from the object of analysis is so great that they are incapable of penetrating or contemplating it, and therefore of knowing it. They cannot fathom the mysteries of life.

The French writer Ernest Renan, author of the world best-seller *The Life of Jesus* (1863), was one of those whose intellect smothered his heart. Renan is not interested in the *object* of knowledge. He is interested in the *knowledge* of the object. He is not interested in Christ; he is interested in knowledge *about* Christ. No more than the mystery of life and the universe does he perceive the mystery of Christ. Renan's overstimulated intellect shrinks and hardens his heart. He cannot grasp the essence of things. Obsessed by the knowledge about Christ, Renan wants to "demystify" the Gospels, but in "demystifying" them, he unconsciously remakes Christ in his own image. He elaborates in his imagination a legend he talks himself into believing. In Renan, the intellect atrophies the heart, and the heart, revolting, speaks of exclusively sentimental things intended for "old people without teeth who like nothing better than pureed turnips."[1]

---

1. Paul Claudel, *Lettre a H. Massis du 10 juillet 1923* in "*Table ronde,*" April 1955. Centre Jacques-Petit de l'Université de Besançon, Annales littéraires de l'Université de Besançon, n°178, Les Belles Lettres, 1975.

The Russian philosopher Pavel Florensky (1882–1937) rightly said, "the essence of true perception is to enter into the profundity of things, whereas the essence of illusory perception is to hide oneself from reality."[2] Renan hides and protects himself from Christ rather than try to penetrate his mystery. To reinvent Christ is probably the best way to protect yourself from him.

Contemplate Velázquez's *Christ on the Cross*. The face of the Crucified is partly obscured by his hair, which falls straight down. The struggle was hard. The Son of Man is dead, but still he speaks to us. He tells us not to be afraid of sorrow, because it is the touchstone of love. Renan, suffocated by what he calls "reason," does not allow himself to be touched, surprised, stunned. He is "too mature, too adult, too autonomous" for anything like that.

Or consider the *Last Supper* of Giotto. The head of Saint John the Apostle reposes on the breast of Christ. The disciple Christ loved is drowning in the ocean of divine mercy. It is a heart-to-heart of extraordinary intensity. Again, Renan does not allow himself to be moved.

---

2. Pavel Florensky, Letter of May 13, 1937, to his daughter Olga from the Solovki concentration camp several months before his execution. Mysl: Moscow, 1998, p. 703.

Rationalism not stirred. *Christ on the Cross* (detail), *Velázquez, Prado Museum, Madrid.*

Instead of experiencing the divine, Renan reduces the divine to his own measure. And the noble Christ of the Gospels becomes the "nice" Christ of Renan.

It is often the case that intellectuals of vast intelligence are aware of the disproportionate role intellect plays in their lives. The French philosopher Jacques Maritain, born into a Protestant Parisian family, and his wife Raïssa Oumansoff, born into a Russian Jewish family, are a good example.

In 1901, during their studies at the Sorbonne, Raïssa and Jacques felt empty and desperate, asphyxiated by the prevalent scientism.[3] In her famous book, *We Have Been Friends Together*, Raïssa recalls:

> We decided for some time to again trust the unknown; we were going to give credence to existence, as to an experiment to be made, in the hope that at our vehement call the meaning of life would be unveiled, that new values would reveal themselves so clearly that they would gain our full support, and would free us from the nightmare of a sinister and pointless world. That if this experiment did not succeed, the solution would be suicide; suicide before the years had accumulated their dust, before our youthful strength had been worn out.

---

3. Scientism is an ideology that regards science as a religion.

> We wanted to die by a free refusal if it was impossible to live according to the truth.[4]

Under the influence of the writer Charles Péguy and the philosopher Henri Bergson, Jacques and Raïssa began to perceive a meaning to their lives.

In her intimate diary, Sophie Scholl, the German anti-Nazi resistance figure who was arrested and executed in 1943, takes up these words of Jacques Maritain: "One must have a hard spirit and a soft heart. Excepting weak spirits with dry hearts, the world is made up mostly of hard spirits with dry hearts and soft hearts with weak spirits."[5]

Renan was a hard spirit with a dry heart. Jacques and Raïssa could have followed his example. But at the crossroads of life they decided to take a very different path, one which Pascal had already taken: "We know the truth not only by reason but also by the heart," he says.

> However powerless we are to prove certain things by reason, this powerlessness only demonstrates the weakness

---

4. Raïssa Maritain, *We Have Been Friends Together* (South Bend: St. Augustine's Press, 2016), p. 70.

5. Jacques Maritain, *Réponse à Jean Cocteau* in *Œuvres complètes de Jacques et Raïssa Maritain*, ed. les Éditions St-Paul, Paris, 1985, vol. III, p. 724.

of our reason, not the uncertainty of all of our knowledge. . . . Likewise, it is as useless and absurd for reason to demand from the heart proofs of the things it knows before consenting to them, as it would be for the heart to demand from reason feelings about all of its demonstrated propositions before accepting them.[6]

If you seek mathematical certainty through the heart, you will be disappointed, just as you would be if you were to seek feelings in reason. Truths of the heart—the intuitive truths—are often more certain than rational truths, even if mathematically demonstrable. But above all, and this is the important thing, they are nearly always more fundamental and contribute more to our happiness and personal growth.

Consideration

Let yourself be touched by the beautiful and the good without trying to reduce them to your poor understanding of realities which are beyond you. You will only understand reality when you quit wanting to "comprehend," contain, and possess it. Let yourself be astonished, thrilled, embraced by that which is greater than you.

---

6. Blaise Pascal, *Pensées*, Paris: Gallimard, vol. II, pp. 573–574.

Judith, the balanced voluntarist. *Judith Beheading Holofernes* (detail), Caravaggio, Galleria Nazionale d'Arte Antica at Palazzo Barberini, Rome.

CHAPTER 4

The Religious Voluntarist

The heart is as prone to being smothered by the will as it is by the intellect. One meets people with excellent intentions who are convinced of the need to stifle their hearts so as to augment the moral value of their will. They aim to banish from their behavior any sort of affectivity so that only the will remains. They even like to act contrary to their heart's inclinations. They have no need of feelings. All they need is a "categorical imperative."

This vision of moral perfection has done much harm to Christianity: Christianity, which is above all the affirmation of the freedom of the children of God—an affirmation directed to the heart of the person—is perceived by many as a compilation of rules to which the will must coldly submit.

But man is called to do good, not only through his will, but also with his heart: with his feelings, his emotions, and his flesh. He is called to savor the good.

The eastern Nirvana and the Stoic apathy, Kantian moralism and Calvinist Puritanism, make no allowance for the role of emotions and feelings in human life. Those who do not perceive the ontological and existential value of their emotions and feelings will never attain excellence. A person's value depends on the quality of his affectivity, and not on his ability to subsume his affectivity to his will.

To grasp what we mean by a stifled heart, one can compare English literature of the Elizabethan period, such as Shakespeare, Spencer, and Sydney (1558–1603), to Calvinist puritanical literature (1625–1675). The former is full of heart, vitality, and hope; the latter is notably intellectual, sad, and pessimistic.

Compare the canvasses of the Puritan period in America and Caravaggio's painting of Judith done several decades earlier, in 1599. The Puritan paintings are dry. Caravaggio's Judith is effervescent, passionate, fleshly. The breast, the mouth, the nose, the eyes reflect the concentration of vital energy the body needs to accomplish the noble and difficult task of beheading Holofernes, the enemy of the Jewish people. Judith is a profoundly corporal being; she is not diminished, frustrated, or alienated.

A striking example of religious voluntarism is the young Calvinist pastor St. John Rivers in Charlotte Brontë's *Jane Eyre*. Rivers, although in love with Rosamund, asks Jane's hand in marriage, because he is convinced she will be a more suitable partner for a missionary. Rivers does not love Jane, nor does she love him; he cares neither about Jane's heart nor his own. Jane hesitates, but at the moment of accepting his proposal, her heart rebels: the voice of the one she *does* love—Rochester—resonates in the depths of her being. Jane does not marry Rivers. She will not sacrifice herself for religion against the deepest inclinations of her heart.

When one stifles the heart, the will sooner or later breaks. The human will is neither a turbojet, nor an army tank. It is rooted in the heart, which is the center of the personality. The heart gives the will direction. Without this direction, all acts of the will are nothing but a dodge, an evasion, a headlong rush over a precipice. Duty for duty's sake is an inhuman notion that often results in a split personality.

The solidity of our virtues depends on the purity of our heart, more than on the strength of our will.

Everyone seeking his or her way in life should remember these things and ask himself: "What, finally, in the core of my being, attracts me? What do I want more than anything?" You cannot base your life on something that is not you, in the name of a duty or moral obligation which exists only in your imagination.

Consideration

Learn to do what you want to do. Learn to be happy. Be convinced that happiness is not a sin!

CHAPTER 5

The Macho Voluntarist

Macho voluntarism takes place when people have an exclusively masculine perception of existence.

Hippocrates outlined 2,500 years ago the four temperaments: the choleric, the melancholic, the sanguine, and the phlegmatic. The choleric and phlegmatic temperaments are rather masculine; the melancholic and sanguine more feminine. The former are rational and willful; the latter are intuitive and warm.[1]

Persons of choleric temperament (and to a lesser degree those of phlegmatic temperament) often believe melancholic

---

1. See Alexandre Havard, *From Temperament to Character: On Becoming a Virtuous Leader* (New York: Scepter, 2019).

and sanguine people need to become more virile. They forget that in ancient Greece melancholy was considered an honor: "All melancholics, said Aristotle, are remarkable people, not by virtue of a disease, but by nature."[2]

Macho voluntarists lack no shortage of examples: Latin Americans (many of whom are sanguine) perceive Spaniards (many of whom are choleric) as macho. While Spaniards see South Americans as sentimentalists who need to be masculinized, the Latino sees Spaniards as voluntarists who need to be softened and humanized.

In any case, an exclusively masculine perception of existence is often the root cause of an inappropriate voluntarism. The macho voluntarist stifles his heart—and that of others—because he is ashamed of it. He feels ashamed of having feelings and feels uneasy around those who do. He is afraid of looking like a sentimentalist. He is afraid not to be macho. And he corrects those he perceives as effeminate sentimentalists.

Beyond the problem posed by confusing feelings with being effeminate, the danger of this approach is obvious: the education of the heart is not a priority for such persons. Instead they prioritize the education of the intellect and the will.

---

2. Aristotle, *Problems*, Volume 2 (Cambridge: Harvard University Press, 1953), p. 150.

This exclusively masculine approach to perfection produces people who appear strong but are, in reality, weak. If you are ashamed to have feelings, you will end up by not having them. And you will wind up without a heart. And without a heart, the will exhausts itself.

Religious voluntarism is the result of a specific upbringing, whereas macho voluntarism is the fruit of a specific culture.

Consideration

Quit thinking that virility and sensitivity are incompatible realities. Quit confusing sensitivity with sentimentalism. Quit being ashamed of your feelings and those of others. Ditch this inappropriate reserve which paralyzes you.

CHAPTER 6

The Ideological Voluntarist

In 1992 in Saint Petersburg, I made the acquaintance of Misha, one of my Georgian cousins. He introduced me to his Russian wife, Valentina. Misha and Valentina had served the Communist Party for several decades. They both taught social psychology at the university level in the former Leningrad.

Misha, a big-hearted man, was probably also an opportunist. He moved to Leningrad after the war, married a girl from the city, and joined the Party. Valentina, for her part, had believed in the system. She gave it her heart.

During our conversation, Misha admitted to me that until not so long ago the police would regularly send him lists of students who should be expelled from the university for their religious views. Valentina exploded: "You don't have to tell Alex about *things like that!*"

Misha speaks about "things like that" because, for him, they are not of a personal or intimate kind: he knew he acted badly, but it seemed to him he had no choice.

But for Valentina, these things revealed intimacies: she did evil not to obey, but out of conviction, out of love, in the name of a radiant future in which she believed. Ideology had taken the place of conscience.

Valentina ended by going insane. I visited her often after Misha died. She spoke to me about Stalin as one speaks about Jesus Christ. Her grandson, Maksim, could not abide her presence. She liked to receive me. I believe that in her state she saw me as an anchor to reality.

Ideological voluntarism devours the heart of those who get tangled up in its web, but its greatest victims are generous hearts devoid of wisdom: they give themselves entirely, generously, to a process leading to their own destruction.

A visual expression of this voluntarism shows in the statue *Worker and Kolkhoz Woman* (1937) by Vera Mukhina. It consists of a manual worker (with hammer in hand) and a female collective farmer (brandishing a sickle). With arms raised and intertwined, they stride decisively toward Communism's radiant future. Over 80 feet high and weighing 80 tons, this monumental sculpture was built for the Universal Exposition of 1937 in Paris.

Worker and Kolkhoz Woman is a hymn to ideology and the human will. The Worker and the Kolkhoz Woman certainly have a heart, but it is absorbed in their omnipotent will. This hymn to ideology is, in fact, a cruel critique of ideology, whether socialist or liberal. The will of the Kolkhoz Woman is at this point in hypertrophy; her body no longer resembles that of a woman: she has become transgendered.

This statue is a brilliant symbol not only of an era, but of a new age that flouts the nature of things, the laws of creation, and the voice of God in man. This master work is the symbol not of a country, but of a planet whose inhabitants flail and struggle in a civilization which has buried its heart and has no other idea than submission to ideological slogans.

Or consider Javert, the police inspector in Victor Hugo's novel, *Les Misérables*. Javert is a man without a heart, an ideologized man from head to toe. Javert is a system more than a person. And when he perceives the forgiveness which Jean Valjean offers him, he rejects the opportunity to free his heart and drowns himself in the Seine.

Consideration

Renounce ideology. Distinguish between the partial truth it contains and the hidden distortion it represents. Contemplate the millions of innocent victims which ideology inexorably produces. Rediscover the nature of things. Marvel at the dignity of the human being. Conscious of past errors, we should not sink into hopelessness or bitterness. Set out again with a new purpose and a resurrected heart.

CHAPTER 7

The Conventional Voluntarist

In addition to religious, macho, and ideological voluntarism, there exists a fourth form of voluntarism: conventional voluntarism.

There are many people whose behavior is conditioned not by the immutable principles of human nature (conscience, virtue), but by social rules.

For these people there are no good actions (those which favor virtue, excellence, and human perfection) or bad (those which are an obstacle to the same): there are only correct actions (those which conform to rules), and incorrect ones (those which do not).

The conventional voluntarist is convinced of his moral perfection: by observing the rules, he accomplishes his duty.

In the novel *Thérèse Desqueyroux*,[1] François Mauriac, recipient of the Nobel Prize for literature, offers an example of a conventional voluntarist in Bernard, the husband of Thérèse.

Bernard is a heartless man who sacrifices everything—including the life and happiness of his wife—to the "interests of the family." This rule—the "interests of the family"—knows no exception. Bernard is incapable of loving Thérèse. Thérèse exists for him only to the extent she can bear in her womb the heir, the progenitor, who will guarantee the interests of the family in the future.

Bernard does not practice virtue (wisdom, self-mastery, justice), but he is convinced of his moral integrity because he fulfills in every instance what the rules prescribe. He creates a scandal in a theater in Paris because the play he is attending seems to him obscene, and shortly thereafter, he tries to force his wife to submit to abuse that is the fruit of his perverse imagination. Bernard has a very precise vision of what is permitted and what is not permitted by the rules. Bernard knows only the rules. He is incapable of

---

1. François Mauriac, *Thérèse Desqueyroux* (New York: Boni & Liveright, 1928).

loving. Upon taking leave of Thérèse, he gets angry with himself for having felt some emotions, for his sadness.

The fundamental problem of the conventional voluntarist is that he does not love. This absence of love renders him blind. He grasps at the rules because these are his only means of support, the only reference point in his life.

Consideration

Learn to love people more than rules, more than traditions, more than the religiously, culturally, or politically correct. Learn to discover the person in every human being. Learn then to sacrifice with joy for the ones you love.

CHAPTER 8

The Voluptuous Sentimentalist

Learning to allow yourself to be moved by noble values and learning not to be ashamed of your emotions, that is the starting point.

It is incorrect to accuse someone of "sentimentalism" for the reason that one is moved by beauty or by the heroic practice of virtue. To have a sensitive heart and to be "sentimental" are two quite different things.

Sentimentalism is not the capacity to be moved emotionally: it is the tendency to enjoy emotions more than the values that give rise to them, to seek out, even wallow in, emotion for the pleasure it brings, to isolate emotion from the good that produced it. Sentimentalism is a form of voluptuousness, of sensuality. It shows in several ways.

He who habitually takes refuge in reading, in movies or music to enjoy the emotions these activities can produce, rather than to imbibe the values they have to offer, is a voluptuous sentimentalist.

He who throws himself into the creation of businesses to enjoy the action and movement that go with it rather than the values which enterprise creates and the virtues it fosters is a voluptuous sentimentalist.

He who practices charity not out of love for people but to feel good about himself is a voluptuous sentimentalist.

He who habitually takes refuge in prayer to feel an emotion such as consolation rather than to experience a personal encounter with God is a voluptuous sentimentalist.

To repeat: to feel emotions is not sentimentalism. Sentimentalism is the isolation of the emotion from the value which produced it. Many politicians' voices tremble with emotion when they pronounce the word "humanity," while the image they have of themselves, to say nothing of the image they have of others, is, in the best of cases, that of a civilized orangutan or of a house pet. Georges Clemenceau, French prime minister during the First World War, was an expert in the subject. The emotional tremor of the voice of the godless humanist is purely physiological in nature. He enjoyed hearing himself speak of exalted matters, but his enjoyment was not spiritual: it was, pure and simple, voluptuousness.

The voluptuous sentimentalist should learn to establish—or re-establish—the connection between emotion and values. To do so, he should learn to contemplate any given value with great sincerity. He should learn to love the value for itself, and to discover its intrinsic beauty. The resulting emotion will be superior in quality to the one he felt before. Joy—and not just pleasure—will become an integral part of his way.

Consideration

Learn to love the good for itself and not just for the pleasure it gives. Examine your conscience. What are you seeking? What deeply motivates your actions? If pleasure, for whatever reason, vanishes, do you persevere in your good actions?

CHAPTER 9

The Insane Sentimentalist

Another form of sentimentalism allows the heart to smother the intellect. Sentimentalism in this sense is a form of insanity.

A powerful intellect is a good thing provided it does not stifle the heart. By the same token, a sensitive heart is a good thing provided it does not stifle the intellect. The heart cannot substitute for the intellect.

The heart knows things which the intellect does not necessarily know. It knows in a more mysterious—and often more ambiguous—way. There are people who consider their heart to be their only guide. Such a heart is, in fact, an arbitrary heart which calls "intuition" that which is the pure product of the imagination and fantasy and nothing else. Before confiding in your heart, you must learn to practice the virtue of prudence (or practical wisdom) in which the heart, the intellect, and the will work hand in hand. Many are those who commit horrendous crimes "in the name of the heart": adultery, sodomy, war, terrorism.

The French philosopher Jean-Jacques Rousseau is a good example of an insane sentimentalist. Convinced he was doing the right thing, he sent his children to the Paris Foundling Hospital immediately upon birth. Rousseau never examined his conscience about what is right and wrong. His only point of reference was his heart, his perverted heart. He "felt" it was right to act this way. Rousseau wrote a lot about justice, but being an insane sentimentalist, he could not practice the virtue of justice, which requires practical wisdom.

The insane sentimentalist likes to cite the celebrated phrase of Pascal: "The heart has its reasons which reason knows not."[1] He forgets that Pascal not only had a big heart but also a refined conscience and an extraordinary moral sensibility. For people devoid of wisdom, it is obvious that the only law should be not that of the

---

1. Pascal, *Pensées*, p. 120.

heart, as they call it, but that of the conscience. The insane sentimentalist is offended at the drop of a hat. He feels offended, but he never questions his intellect to know if this feeling is the result of a real and objective offense. "I feel offended," he says, and that is enough for him to make war on the whole world.

The insane sentimentalist is not a person of heart, but rather a fool who is manipulated by his or her egoism and pride. Insane sentimentalism is where the heart goes to die. Insane sentimentalism is a disease widespread in the modern world.

Consideration

Learn to listen to your conscience before listening to what you call "your heart." The voice of your conscience, which is the voice of God, has priority over the voice of your "I." A heart separated from its conscience in not a free heart. It is a perverted, self-centered, hypocritical heart.

CHAPTER 10

The Cowardly Sentimentalist

Sentimentalism is sometimes voluptuous, sometimes insane. It can also be cowardly. Numerous are those who, "out of love for others," refuse to confront them when they need to be put back on the right track.

The cowardly sentimentalist will not correct his child, his student, his employee, or his friend on the pretext that one must not cause others to suffer. He fears the confrontation, even if it is constructive. He is devoid of courage. His will has been absorbed by his heart. The cowardly sentimentalist has a heart too "good" to be able to do good, a heart too "loving" to be able to love.

Ivan Turgenev's *Rudin* is profoundly sentimental. Capable of passion, and of stoking up the passion of others through his enthusiastic discourses on liberty, sacrifice, and action, he inflames hearts but is incapable of action. The young Natalia is in love with him. She is captivated by his ideals. But then Natalia tells Rudin her mother said she would rather see her dead than married to him.

Rudin asks her what she said in reply. "I said I would rather die than marry anyone else." Natalia is ready to break her ties with her family in order to go with Rudin. She asks him if he has a plan. And this is how our hero replied: we should separate because your "mother does not agree."

Rudin has feelings, but he does not have the will to confront his future mother-in-law. He does not want her to suffer. It is almost laughable—Rudin tries to justify his attitude to Natalia, but in the depth of his being he knows he is useless, a nobody: "Nature has given me many talents, but I will die without ever having accomplished anything. . . . The first obstacle . . . and I fall apart . . . I spin my wheels, that's the way I am. I will end badly."[1]

---

1. Ivan Turgenev, *Rudin*, *www.gutenberg.org*, The Project Gutenberg EBook of Rudin, by Ivan Turgenev, Last Updated: October 26, 2016.

"Mother does not agree!" The cowardly sentimentalist must make his will more masculine and learn to practice the virtue of courage.

Consideration

Strengthen your will. Do not renounce the good on the pretext that it could be a source of conflict. Learn to manage conflicts with sincerity and firmness.

CHAPTER 11

Desiccated Hearts

We have spoken of **unbalanced hearts** whose poor functioning stems from their lack of communion and interaction with the intelligence and the will. Now we must talk about desiccated hearts: hearts insensitive to beauty, virtue, love, greatness, mercy, and the pain of others.

One example is demonic hearts like those of Dostoevsky's *The Possessed* who are always prepared, with unparalleled cynicism, to tear down the most noble things in life. The dramatic events of recent centuries confirm the existence of such hearts:

> "Listen. We are going to make a revolution," Pierre Verkhovensky muttered rapidly, almost in a delirium

[. . .] "We are going to make such an upheaval that everything will be uprooted from its foundation [. . .] Every member of society spies on the others, and it's his duty to inform against them. Everyone belongs to all and all to everyone [. . .] Equality must reign in a herd [. . .] We will stifle every genius in its infancy [. . .] Slaves must have masters [. . .] Absolute submission, absolute loss of individuality, but once every thirty years, they would all suddenly begin eating one another up, to a certain point, simply as a precaution to boredom [. . .] On all sides we see vanity puffed up out of all proportion; monstrous appetites without precedent [. . .] Unparalleled debauchery, vile, dirty [. . .] There's going to be such an upset that the world has never seen before. In this we have a force, and what a force! We need only one lever to lift up the earth. Everything will rise up. And the sea will rise up and the whole gimcrack show will fall to the ground, and then we shall consider how to build up an edifice of stone. For the first time! *We* are going to build it and only we!"[1]

Dostoevsky's possessed souls are desperate people, truly devoid of hope. They do not believe in God but in the

---

1. Fyodor Dostoevsky, *The Possessed* (New York: Barnes & Noble Classics, 2004), p. 130, Part II, Chapter VIII.

devil. In their despair, they decide to blow up the world so that they can build a new one in their own image, something new and impossible to imagine: an earthly hell, eternal and indestructible.

These hearts, which are out of control, roam the earth seeking to transform it into a hell. Only exorcism fixes them. Such hearts exist but they are the exception. More numerous are desiccated hearts like Flaubert's Frédéric Moreau,[2] Lermontov's Grigory Pechorin,[3] Pushkin's Eugene Onegin[4] and Mauriac's Isabelle Fondaudège.[5] These hearts sank very low because they tried to stifle the voice of their own conscience.

Frédéric Moreau is a young man with romantic ideas during the Second French Empire (1852–1870). He abandons himself to superficiality and cynicism. Flaubert's *Sentimental Education* is a work on how to "get rid" of one's education.

Grigory Pechorin is a jaded aristocrat incapable of feeling anything. He ruins the life of everyone he encounters.

---

2. Gustave Flaubert, *Sentimental Education*, *www.gutenberg.org*, Last updated: December 24, 2011.

3. Mikhail Lermontov, *A Hero of Our Time*, *www.gutenberg.org*, Last updated: November 10, 2016.

4. Alexander Pushkin, *Eugene Onegin* (Oxford University Press: 1998).

5. François Mauriac, *Vipers' Tangle* (Chicago: Loyola Classics, 2005).

He is a man whose "eyes never laughed when he laughed."[6] But Grigory Pechorin is deeper and more honest than Frédéric Moreau:

> For what purpose was I born? . . . A purpose there must have been, and, surely, mine was an exalted destiny, because I feel that within my soul are powers immeasurable. . . . But I was not able to discover that destiny, I allowed myself to be carried away by the allurements of passions, inane and ignoble.[7]

The perverse inclinations of human nature, if left unchecked, stifle the heart even more than they harm the intellect and the will. Obsessed by his power, his possessions, and his pleasures, the intemperate person conceives of life as an accumulation of sensations. He no longer notices others—their dignity, their sorrows, their needs.

Eugene Onegin is a disenchanted nobleman who thinks only of himself. He leads an idle life and, to amuse himself, seduces the fiancée of his best friend, then kills the latter in a duel.

---

6. Mikhail Lermontov, *A Hero of Our Time*, *www.gutenberg.org*, Last Updated: November 10, 2016, Chapter XVIII.

7. Lermontov, *A Hero of Our Time*.

François Mauriac's Isabelle Fondaudège claims to be practicing her faith but never questions the order of things—often hypocritical and unjust—established by her social class. "I have never known anyone more serenely unjust than you," declares her husband, Louis. "God knows what little sins you confess. And there is not a single one of the Beatitudes you have not spent your life contradicting."[8] Isabelle is a woman whose heart is desiccated, a Pharisee who willingly confesses her minor faults, without ever noticing that her entire being is sin. Each act is perverted by the immoral nature of her motives, with a moral superiority typical of the self-righteous. For Isabelle, fulfilling the outward requirements of Christian practice absolves her of having to live in a Christian way. It seems Isabelle has fallen even lower than Moreau or Pechorin.

Each one of these people has freely become what he or she is. They did not begin this way. No heart is dry from birth. It becomes dry. Where does this dryness come from? It is the fruit of selfish choices, which make one impenetrable to transcendence and alienated from others.

The choices we make from early childhood clearly depend on the values of parents, teachers and those around

---

8. Mauriac, *Vipers' Tangle*, p. 160.

us. But these choices are, in the last analysis, *our* choices, it is *we* who make them, consciously or unconsciously.

Desiccated hearts are not necessarily lost. They are cold hearts that must melt in the warm tears of conversion. The depraved Grigory Pechorin could have converted his heart in contact with the chaste Princess Meri, who was madly in love with him. The very selfish Eugene Onegin might have understood the horror of his condition through contact with the generous Tatiana who desperately loved him. The very hypocritical Isabelle Fondaudège might have succeeded in overcoming her blindness if she had not preceded her husband in death and had read the sincere confession he addressed to her.

Consideration

To cure a desiccated heart, you must tackle it with all the power of your patience and your love. You must push it to be sincere.

CHAPTER 12

Wounded Hearts

Desiccated hearts are responsible for their own degradation, which is not the same as wounded hearts who were victims of external aggression. The most deeply wounded hearts are those that were hurt by those who should have loved them.

Anton Chekhov's novella, *Three Years*, tells of the two Laptev brothers, Aleksei and Fyodor, the sons of a Moscow businessman, as they discuss the meaning of life. It is a dialogue of cruel sincerity in which Aleksei reveals the nature of the war he wages against himself to regain his dignity. Fyodor has just written a tract on the greatness of Russia and the misery of Europe. Aleksei accuses him of having lost his senses.

They were silent for a minute. Fyodor sighed and said:

"It's an immense regret to me, dear brother, that we think differently. Oh, Alyosha, Alyosha, my dear brother! You and I are true Russians, true believers, men of broad nature, all of these ideas are not for us. You and I are not wretched upstarts, you know, but representatives of a distinguished merchant family."

"What do you mean by a distinguished family?" said Aleksei, restraining his irritation. "A distinguished family! The landowners beat our grandfather and every low little government clerk punched him in the face. Our grandfather thrashed our father, and our father thrashed us. What has your distinguished family done for us? What sort of nerves, what sort of blood, have we inherited?

For nearly three years you've been arguing like an ignorant deacon, and talking all sorts of nonsense, and now you've written this slavish drivel here! While I, while I! Look at me . . . No elasticity, no boldness, no strength of will; I tremble over every step I take as though I should be flogged for it. I am timid before nonentities, idiots, brutes, who are immeasurably my inferiors mentally and morally; I am afraid of porters, doorkeepers, policemen, gendarmes. I am afraid of everyone, because

I was born of a mother who was terrified, and because from a child I was beaten and frightened! . . . You and I will do well to have no children. Oh, God, grant that this distinguished merchant family may die with us!"[1]

What saves Aleksei Laptev is his sincerity, his self-knowledge, and his desire to live an entirely new life. Fyodor, self-deceived and alienated, winds up living out his last days in an asylum. But will Aleksei be able to go all the way? Will he be able to pardon his father from the bottom of his heart, and thus definitively heal his still-open wound?

This chapter on wounded hearts may seem to be inordinately short. But Chekhov, whose novel is heavily autobiographical, said *everything* in a few lines.

Consideration

Wounds inflicted by one's own family are wounds which only forgiveness can definitively cure.

---

1. Anton Chekhov, *Three Years*, in *The Darling and Other Stories* (Frankfurt am main: Outlook, 2018), p. 154, Chapter XV.

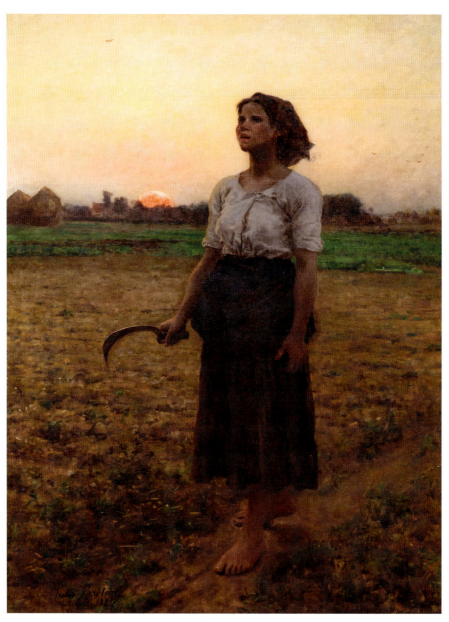

Beauty does not leave the heart unstirred. *The Song of the Lark*, Jules Breton, Art Institute of Chicago.

CHAPTER 13

Beauty

Thus far, we have considered how unbalanced hearts can achieve equilibrium, how desiccated hearts can find new life, how wounded hearts can be healed. Now, we need to turn our attention to the education of the heart, the enhancement of our affectivity, and letting our most noble sentiments reach an exalted level of strength and maturity.

If we wish to give rein to our most noble feelings, we must learn to experience beauty, greatness, love, freedom, mercy, and suffering.

For Plato, everything that is true, beautiful, and good in the world is only the reflection of an archetype, of a divine ideal which we cannot appreciate here below. Only beauty delights us to the point of freeing us from the world's grip, from a humdrum environment, and from things that control us. The contemplation of beauty, Plato tells us, makes us nostalgic for another world. This contemplation of beauty—the delight and the ecstasy it causes—also makes us "lovers." It gives us wings, it elevates us, it deifies us. This ecstasy is not directed towards immediate pleasure, but offers something superior to bodily satisfaction.

Beauty is found on faces, in nature, and in art. Genuine masterpieces, such as books, paintings, songs, and films, provoke in us emotions capable of lifting us to unsuspected heights. In euphoric amazement, we shed our self-satisfaction and mediocrity. These works communicate the beauty and greatness of the human being and awaken a thirst for life, for accomplishing things and for sacrificing ourselves.

Consider the canvas *Song of the Lark* (1882) by Jules Breton, at the Art Institute of Chicago. A young peasant woman, struck by the song of the lark, interrupts her work at sunrise. She is surprised and amazed by the song's beauty, although she probably hears it every day. For her, miracles are ordinary. It reminds us that, like the lark song, everything is a gift, a miracle, and nothing proceeds from itself. Her free heart responds instinctively to the call of beauty. She contemplates. Her response is a "yes" of extraordinary intensity. She gives herself over to it. She is transformed, almost transfigured by the experience.

The *Song of the Lark* cannot leave our hearts indifferent. One grasps a great deal in the blinking of an eye. Beauty is imbued with the true and the good. One cannot *not* respond. I understand why the American actor Bill Murray, who had a hard time starting out in the 1970s in Chicago and was tempted to take his own life, gave up the idea after seeing this painting.

Then we can consider the lines of the songs of Jacques Brel:

If we only have love / To live our promises / Without any other riches / Except to always believe . . . If we only have love / To make our way / And change the course of fate / At every crossroads. . . .[1]

I will offer you / Pearls of rain / Come from lands / Where it does not rain . . . I will dig up the earth /

---

1. Jacques Brel, *Quand on n'a que l'amour* (English: *When love is all you have*), the original album was released in April 1957 by Philips (N76.085R). "Quand on n'a que l'amour / Pour vivre nos promesses / Sans nulle autre richesse / Que d'y croire toujours . . . Quand on n'a que l'amour / Pour tracer un chemin / Et forcer le destin / À chaque carrefour. . . ."

*Until after I die / To cover your body / With gold and light . . . I will establish a realm / Where love will be king / Where love will be law / Where you will be queen. . . .*²

Brel lost the God of his childhood, but the echoes of His voice continued to resonate in his heart. Few love songs are as sincere, as intense, and as poetic as those of Brel. His aesthetic sensibility causes the heart to take flight.

God speaks to us through beauty. But God is not a tyrant: he wants us to adhere freely to the values he offers us and let us be penetrated and joyously transformed by them. Nature, literature, painting, music, and film produce feelings that elevate, purify, and transfigure the heart. It's about spontaneous and radically personal experiences: God speaks to each one of us in a language we know and in circumstances that make us particularly receptive.

---

2. Jacques Brel, *Ne Me Quitte Pas* (English: Don't leave me) Released in 1972 by Barclay (80145). "Je creuserai la terre / Jusqu'après ma mort / Pour couvrir ton corps / D'or et de lumière. / Je ferai un domaine / Où l'amour sera roi / Où l'amour sera loi / Où tu seras reine. . . ."

These experiences, if we do not remain indifferent to them, expand and strengthen the heart.

We should trust in beauty. A humble heart, a heart attentive to the voice of conscience, is not afraid of beauty. He knows he can find there the nourishment that gives life, the fuel that lets him soar.

Sergei Bulgakov, the Russian philosopher and theologian, was a Marxist before returning to the Christianity of his childhood. In 1898 in the Dresden Art Gallery, he went through a conversion while he was contemplating the famous *Sistine Madonna* of Raphael:

> On a misty fall morning, we hastened to make a quick visit, as tourists must do, to the Zwinger with its famous gallery. I had no competence in art at all, and I certainly had no idea what awaited me in that gallery.
>
> And that is where the Queen of Heaven entered my soul, coming on clouds with the pre-eternal Infant. Her eyes conveyed purity of great strength, the clear vision of the sacrifice she would have to make; she knew she would suffer and she was ready for this voluntary suffering. The same wisdom in accepting sacrifice can be seen in the eyes of the Infant, a wisdom which was not that of a child. They know what awaits them, what they are destined for, and they will freely give themselves over to it,

A Marxist finds faith in beauty. *Raphael's Sistine Madonna*, (detail), *Dresden Art Museum, Germany.*

to accomplish the will of Him who sent them: he on Golgotha and she "to receive the sword that would pierce her heart."

I was not myself, my head was spinning, tears of joy and bitterness, both, flowed from my eyes while the ice melted in my heart and a vital knot came undone. It was not an aesthetic emotion, no, it was an encounter, a new awareness, a miracle . . . I was then a Marxist, but, spontaneously, I called this contemplation "prayer," and, every morning, trying to arrive at the Zwinger before others had gotten there, I rushed to the Madonna to "pray" and cry; few instances in my life will be more blessed than those tears . . . Sistine Mother of God of Dresden, you have touched my heart and it trembles at your call.[3]

As Bulgakov said, his emotion was not aesthetic, but religious. But it is through aesthetics that the religious encounter took place. In the Madonna's face—at once anxious and serene—he discovered the meaning of his own existence. His cold heart shed, for the first time, the warm tears of repentance and gratitude.

---

3. Sergei Bulgakov, *Unfading Light* (Grand Rapids: Eerdmans Publishing, 2012), pp. 8–9.

Twenty-six years later in 1924, Bulgakov again stood before the *Sistine Madonna*, but this time the encounter left him cold. His initial ecstatic reaction was no longer in evidence. Disenchantment had set in, which testifies more than anything else to the authenticity of the initial encounter: God speaks to us, not the masterpiece. Beauty is only an instrument. If the work of art today no longer speaks to us, this does not call into question the validity of the transcendent impulses that God caused us to feel—by means of a masterpiece at a given moment in life.

In any case, God often uses the same instrument, the same miracle of beauty, to touch the hearts of many people. It was probably after having contemplated this same face—a copy of the *Sistine Madonna* which he kept with him all his life—that Dostoevsky has Prince Myshkin, the principal character of his novel *The Idiot*, say: "Beauty will save the world." In most of Dostoyevsky's work, the *Sistine Madonna* of Raphael is present in one way or another. In *The Possessed*, she becomes the universal symbol of beauty upon which the nihilists spit their contempt.

Beauty will save the world because it is the most direct and tangible expression of the true and the good. After Descartes, one can doubt everything, except beauty. Beauty is the "flesh" of the true and the good. It imposes itself on our senses. It does not submit to relativistic slogans. The prevailing agnosticism has no hold on it. In a world in which doubt is the supreme value, beauty is a secure port in the storm.

Consideration

Begin at the beginning: create beauty where you live, work, and recreate. Beauty is harmony and dignity, order and rectitude. Beauty is compatible with both poverty and affluence, but it clashes with nastiness and neglect, with bad taste and the spirit of the nouveau-riche. Create around you an atmosphere that transcends, an environment shot through with the true and the beautiful. Your friends will want to visit your home because of the warmth, inspiration, and dignity they find there.

Magnanimity in the face of young Walter Raleigh (left, with arms around his knees). *The Boyhood of Raleigh, John Everett Millais, Tate Gallery, London.*

CHAPTER 14

Greatness

The experience of the good, like the experience of the beautiful, sets the heart in motion. It expands, purifies, and inflames it.

Each one of us could recount adventures that left him deeply shaken and were perhaps the occasion of a radical change in his life. I will never forget the old lady of Vyborg, the provincial capital of Russian Karelia, whom I met one day as she was rummaging through piles of garbage near the main rail station. She bought flowers for me with the rubles I had just given her, even though she was suffering from hunger and cold.[1]

---

1. Alexandre Havard, *Virtuous Leadership* (New York: Scepter, 2008), Foreword.

Generosity, gratitude, audacity—these virtues do not leave our hearts indifferent. But one virtue is more able to inflame our hearts than all the others—magnanimity. According to Aristotle, magnanimity is the virtue of those who believe themselves worthy of great things.[2]

Reflect on this painting by John Everett Millais in which we see two boys—the young Sir Walter Raleigh (1552–1618), the famous Elizabethan Age explorer, and his brother—sit facing a Genoese sailor on a Devonshire beach. As the sailor speaks of his adventures, his right arm is extended towards the sea in a gesture of challenge. Walter, clasping his arms around his knees, is seized by the greatness of adventure and discovery of unknown lands. The dream in his heart becomes mission and reality. He is terrified because he knows there is no going back. His brother, for his part, is indifferent to it all. He listens but he does not hear. He remains calm because adventure has no interest for him. This canvas is an allegory of magnanimity.

Magnanimity is the virtue of excellence: excellence in being and excellence in action. The magnanimous person wants to *do* great things, but he wants above all to *be* great. He has confidence in himself, in his talents, in his capacities. He feels himself to be free and strong. He

---

[2]. Alexandre Havard, *Created for Greatness* (New York: Scepter, 2014), p. 30.

pushes his imagination through to the end. He is full of human hope. He dreams and transforms his dream into a mission. He sees in the great problems of humanity great opportunities. He sees obstacles as summits to be conquered. He is convinced that evil is the good he does not do. His life can be summarized in these words of Padraic Pearse, the Anglo-Irish poet and executed hero of the 1916 Easter Uprising: "Ye shall venture your all, lest ye lose what is more than all."[3]

The greatness of the magnanimous terrifies pusillanimous hearts but emboldens the humble.

Thomas More, the English political leader, refused to allow himself to be manipulated by his king, and sacrificed all—his family, his work, his reputation, even his life—to save the integrity of his conscience....

Aleksandr Solzhenitsyn, the Russian writer, who, in the face of a system of nearly cosmic mendacity, stupidity, cruelty, and destruction, threw himself with confidence into the struggle for the liberation of his people from Communist ideology....

Jérôme Lejeune, the French geneticist who, to defend scientific truth about the commencement of human life and the moral truth which flows from it, sacrificed

---

3. Padraic Pearse, *The Fool*, in Collected Works of Pádraic H. Pearse (New York: AMS Press, 1978) p. 334.

his reputation and career to become the most powerful advocate of the smallest and most vulnerable human beings . . .

Teresa of Calcutta, the Albanian nun, who, consistent with her specific vocation, gave the destitute and abandoned tender care and love in their dying days, resisted calls as well as large donations to turn her hospice into a clinic to restore them to health . . .

Joan of Arc, the peasant girl of Lorraine, who, at the age of seventeen, transformed a troupe of outlaws into a bold military force and provoked the spiritual renewal of a nation . . .

The education of the heart occurs by experiencing greatness. And usually one discovers greatness through the realities of ordinary life. It suffices to pay attention. Look around you. There is no shortage of magnanimous people: parents, friends, teachers—their life is headline-worthy even if they remain unknown.

Consideration

Identify some magnanimous people you would like to spend time with. Seek out their company. Contemplate them, study them, try to imitate them. Create a "magnanimous environment" around yourself. Your environment consists of the books you read, the movies you watch, the music you listen to; also, the internet with all that is worthwhile and tawdry. Be selective, reject the morally dubious, and fill your heart and your mind with the noble and beautiful.

Love in a child's adoring look. *Returning from the City* (detail), *Aleksei Korzukhin*.

CHAPTER 15

Love

Contemplate the canvas by Aleksei Korzukhin, *Returning from the City* (1870). Here the father of modest family returns home from work. He is exhausted; his eyes red with fatigue. Nevertheless, he does not rest, drink, or eat. He hands his little daughter a toy he has just bought. She gazes into his face with limitless devotion. This painting depicts the greatness and heroism of ordinary life.

Generous, unconditional love transforms us in the depth of our being. Love is the supreme good when it is given to us by a mother or a father, a brother or a sister, a husband or a wife, a friend or a stranger, by God himself. Then love, if we are disposed to receive it, liberates us from our small-mindedness.

Man was created to be loved, but many are not loved enough. We have spoken of damaged hearts, of wounds which can heal only when we forgive our tormentors. Often, however, we do not perceive the love that is being shown to us, and do not recall the love that was shown to us in the past.

Love is not just the feeling that we are loved, but also the experience of loving someone else.

In the most terrible hours of his life—at Auschwitz—Viktor Frankl, the Austrian psychoanalyst, lovingly thought of the face of his wife. This gave him the strength to resist sinking into despair.[1]

Henri Guillaumet, the French aviator whose plane crashed in June 1930 in the Andes, was tempted to give up and die in the snow. The thought of his wife gave him the courage to survive. He walked for five days and four nights—without food and in subzero temperatures.[2]

Divine love functions according to the same principles as human love. We love God and creatures with one and the same heart. It is impossible to love God with a

---

1. Viktor Frankl, *Man's Search for Meaning* (Boston: Beacon Press, 2006).

2. Antoine de Saint-Exupéry, *Wind, Sand and Stars* (Boston: Mariner Books, 2002).

purely spiritual heart. The Old Testament *Song of Songs* amply confirms this view: love is necessarily rooted in man's physicality, in his or her body. To love God, one must be *in love* with him.

Eros is necessarily present in authentic love. Man is an incarnate being. True love, including supernatural love—that is to say, charity—cannot sustain itself without ecstasy. This ecstasy is the beginning of a voyage which is the gift of self. Authentic *Eros* leads necessarily to *Agape*, to self-sacrifice.

The experience of love, whether human or divine, transforms us into passionate beings, joyous, strong and generous. It makes us fascinating people.

Consideration

Remember those privileged moments when love overtook you and inundated your heart with an intense joy and exalted your dignity. Contemplate those moments of your life. Cleanse your memory of anything that could make you bitter or resentful.

CHAPTER 16

Freedom

The scene of the Grand Inquisitor in Dostoevsky's *The Brothers Karamazov* is one of the most brilliant scenes in world literature. Set in fifteenth century Seville, the author imagines that Jesus has returned to earth to take a close look at the Spanish Inquisition—an episode in history which can hardly be said to have conformed to Christ's teaching. The Grand Inquisitor claps him in chains and condemns him to death.

> Tomorrow I will burn you at the stake. Wasn't it you who said so often at that time, "I want to set you free"? Well, you saw them today, those "free" men. . . . Yes, that case cost us very dearly . . . but, we finally closed it. . . . For fifteen centuries we have tortured

ourselves with this freedom, but now it is over and done with. . . . Know that it is now, yes, at this very moment, when these people have freely offered us their freedom and slavishly set it at our feet, that they are surer than ever of being fully free. . . . Nothing, ever, either for human society or man has been more unbearable than freedom! . . . They know that they can never be free, because they are weak, vicious, rebellious. . . . But only one who can appease their conscience can take over their freedom.

The Inquisitor remains silent; he waits for his prisoner to respond. His silence oppresses him. He saw that the prisoner listened in a subdued and earnest manner looking him straight in the eye, without wanting to say anything in reply. The old man wanted him to say something, even something dreadful or embittered. But, He, suddenly approaches the old man, and, without saying anything kisses his white, nonagenarian lips. That is his response. The old man shudders.

"The kiss scalded his heart."[1]

Reading this account, one understands the whole drama of modern history. It is a history based on an

---

1. Fyodor Dostoevsky, *The Brothers Karamazov* (New York: Farrar, Straus and Giroux, 2002), Part II, Book V, Chapter V, p. 350.

affirmation of unheard-of violence: freedom is a failure! Man has never had any other desire than to satisfy all of his whims without being disturbed for one instant by his conscience!

It is a monstrous libel. The prisoner seems to give in: he does not defend himself, does not justify himself. But with his final gesture, he harrows the Inquisitor's soul: "The kiss scalded his heart."

It is the kiss of God's loving providence: "I want sons and not slaves!" It is the experience of our dignity that allows us to understand and love freedom. Stripped of the status of a child of God, the modern is unable to grasp the meaning of freedom. "It is *now*, yes, at this very moment, when these people have freely offered us their freedom and slavishly set it at our feet, that they are surer than ever of being fully free."

"The truth will make you free," declares Christ.[2] But what truth? The truth of our status as sons and daughters of God. A heart conscious of its dignity is a free heart.

Religion is the most brutal upheaval one can imagine, the most intolerable subversion of all forms of totalitarianism, whether overt or concealed. "Religion," says Saint Josemaría Escrivá,

---

2. Jn 8:32.

is the greatest rebellion of men, who refuse to live like animals, who are dissatisfied and restless until they know their Creator and are on intimate terms with him. . . . Slavery or divine sonship, this is the dilemma we face. Children of God or slaves to pride, to sensuality, to the fretful selfishness which seems to afflict so many souls.[3]

To be a son is to rebel against anything that would dispossess us of our status as son, it is to refuse to belong to the herd, but rather to enroll in an elite corps made up of men and women for whom freedom is more than just a choice between the pathetic options offered to the residents of a fat farm, but consists in voluntarily choosing the good.

So that our affectivity might unfold generously and attain a high degree of power and perfection, we must learn to enjoy our condition as sons of God. We must stop thinking of religion as a superstructure, as an artificial set-piece, as a last-minute addition. Man is a religious being by nature, in the same way as he is, by nature, a social being. The denial of man's natural religiosity, like the denial of his natural sociability, does not stem from

---

3. Josemaría Escrivá, *Friends of God* (New York: Scepter, 1996), no. 38.

science but from ideology. It is a lie that diminishes us, a hoax that degrades the heart.

Consideration

Be conscious of your dignity and assert it. Do not let the businessmen and ideologues of whatever stripe manipulate you, zombify you, turn you into an empty suit, a man without a past, without a country, without a family, and without God. Learn to say "no." Refuse to run with the herd. Cultivate within you a noble and healthy superiority.

Eve's horror at the expulsion from Eden. *The Expulsion of Adam and Eve from Eden* (detail), *Masaccio, church in Italy.*

CHAPTER 17

Mercy

In the fresco by Masaccio (1401–1428), *The Expulsion of Adam and Eve from Eden*, (c. 1424–1427) Adam and Eve are being driven out of Paradise. Eve shows a face of horror. Her heart is devastated. In disobeying God, Eve has lost her dignity, her natural goodness, and her innocence. She grasps in her heart and body the scope of her degradation. Her face displays the whole quantity of rottenness and stupidity which, through her, will be unleashed on humanity until the end of time. She moans over her sin. But she does not know the heart of God, she does not know his mercy. Instead of throwing herself into his paternal arms to ask pardon and to put an end, once and for all, to this miserable story, she retreats into the labyrinth of her sorrow, a sorrow which is not contrition but bitterness.

Sincere contrition is the path to interior peace. Our miseries cease to be a burden. God is a father, and the essence of paternity is to forgive. He forgives sins, even the most egregious ones. But how do you forgive someone who does not ask forgiveness? The only unforgivable sin is not to recognize that one has sinned. This is the sin of the Pharisees.

Contrition is a sublime emotion. The Prodigal Son squanders his inheritance by throwing parties with prostitutes. King David steals Bathsheba, the wife of Uriah the Hittite, the head of his army, and has him killed to cover up his own sin. Both return to their Father with broken hearts.

In a portrait of David by Spanish painter Pedro Berruguete, we see a striking change in David. Once wild and out of control, he takes on the look of a man transformed by the tenderness of God. A shattered heart is the most agreeable offering to God. David is the only person God ever called "a man after my heart."[1]

---

1. Acts 13:22.

David shows the face of mercy in old age. *David, Pedro Berruguete* (1500).

Contrition makes us grow; it also helps us to rebound, as Jacques Brel wrote:

> We have often seen / Fire spurting up / From a defunct volcano / That we considered to be too old. . . . It seems like / Burned earth / Producing more wheat / Than a warm April.[2]

To give more wheat, to give more fire—to transform sin into victory. A contrite heart draws momentum from its failures, strength from its weakness.

The unforgivable sin is to deny one's sins. In fact, there is another type of sin, which could be to doubt God's mercy. That is the sin of Judas Iscariot. Eve did not know the heart of God, but Judas should have known from living three years alongside the God-made-man.

A contrite heart that has been forgiven is a heart at peace with God, with itself, with others. The experience of mercy makes us merciful people. If the experience of our status as sons of God impels us to action and rebellion against sin, the experience of pardon makes us

---

2. Jacques Brel, *Ne me quitte pas*. "On a vu souvent / Rejaillir le feu / D'un ancien volcan / Qu'on croyait trop vieux . . . Il est paraît-il / Des terres brûlées / Donnant plus de blé / Qu'un meilleur avril."

compassionate and understanding towards others, including our enemies. The experience of mercy expands our heart and makes us capable of powerfully experiencing the most exalted emotions of the heart of the God-man.

Consideration

Do not be ashamed of your sins. Do not be afraid of revealing yourself the way you are. Learn sincerity and transparency. Learn to ask forgiveness for your mistakes without delay, and immediately to forgive.

Suffering in the field. *Man with a Hoe*, Jean-François Millet, Getty Museum, Los Angeles.

CHAPTER 18

Suffering

In the painting *Man with a Hoe* (1860–1862) at the Getty Museum in Los Angeles, Jean-François Millet presents a stark image of a peasant of gigantic stature exhausted by his labor in the fields. He supports himself on the shaft of a hoe. His nose is massive. His hands are enormous. His clogs are huge. His back is bent even though he is still young. His face is the color of the earth. His eyes are sunken. He seems to be looking forward, into the distance, but he is really not looking anywhere: he is suffering. This man could be the Christ who bears on his shoulders, with patience and humility, the sins of the world. This man could also be the proletarian of Marx who "has nothing to lose but his chains," or one of those who, in a few years, would "blow up the joint" to use the expression beloved of Dostoevsky's possessed ones. Suffering is the shortest way to heaven. It is also the shortest way to hell. In pain, one needs great humility to make the right choice.

Suffering makes people grow or diminishes them. Coming to terms with suffering and nobly accepting the challenge it represents is the path that leads to happiness. Pierre Bezukhov, Natasha Rostov, and Andrei Bolkonsky—the main characters in Tolstoy's *War and Peace*—are transfigured by suffering. Their transformation is radical and their happiness—in the face of both life and death—is without limit.

Without a religious vision of life, one cannot grasp the ultimate meaning of pain. Varlam Shalamov and Aleksandr Solzhenitsyn both depicted life in Soviet concentration camps, but those depictions differed greatly. Shalamov, an atheist, sees the horror and only the horror. Solzhenitsyn, a believer, discovers greatness. It is the greatness of the man who grasps the existential challenge confronting him and takes it up with head held high and with all the strength of his faith, his hope, and his love.

Suffering is a mystery, a "sacrament." One wants to go down on one's knees before those who have suffered. My grandparents came of age in the Soviet Union. When we were children, we looked on them—my brother, my sister, and I—as superior beings, because we knew they had suffered through the First World War, the Communist Revolution, and the disappearance of their parents and friends in the Russian Civil War. Suffering lent them beauty.

A heart which has suffered with humility and patience is a heart that has been divinized by a supernatural presence, such as Anna Akhmatova experienced: "No, it is not I, it is someone else who is suffering. To suffer in such a way—I would not be able to."[1] In her sorrow—her husband shot to death, her only son in a concentration camp—the Russian poet understood the amplitude of the gift she had received, that it was not she who suffered, but God who suffered in her. Suffering for her is a good deal more than a simple encounter: it is a union, a communion in the very mystery of the life of God.

Man was made to be loved, and it is in suffering that this love, in a mysterious and paradoxical way, is communicated to him most effectively.

---

1. Anna Akhmatova, *Requiem*, III, *https://www.culture.ru/poems/10174/rekviem*.

Suffering plays a privileged role in educating the heart, but the heart must be sufficiently humble and mature to emerge victorious from the ordeal. Suffering is an ultimate, final, eschatological experience: it demands all and takes all. But in this hand-to-hand combat of often unimaginable violence, the heart of man expands and is divinized.

Consideration

Gold is forged in fire. Do not seek pain, but when it presents itself, do not lose your peace. Receive it willingly. Discover its deepest meaning. Love it.

Conclusion

The experience of beauty, greatness, love, freedom, mercy, and suffering expands and exalts our heart. It purifies it and makes it burn.

The only obstacle is pride. A proud heart does not respond to transcendent values. It hears but does not react. And because it does not react, it ceases to hear.

A humble heart is always listening. It is open and receptive. It is full of gratitude. It is happy.

The heart gets formed at a young age. Why is a young girl of four receptive to beauty and love whereas her twin sister seems indifferent to transcendent realities? It is in the intimacy of a child's heart in which the first—often decisive—combat takes place between good and evil, between generosity and selfishness. The most fundamental orientations of our existence are formed in the first years of our life, well before our intelligence is capable of fully functioning.

A humble heart is a heart open to transcendence. A proud heart is a heart closed in on itself. For the humble heart, life is a discovery. For the proud heart, it is nothing but self-assertion.

Humility is the habit of living in the truth and the big truth is that we were created to be loved. Letting God love us is the great challenge of life.